THE POWER OF INDUSTRY

Featuring the story of Benjamin Franklin

Author
Virginia Swenson

Art Illustrator
Stephen P. Krause

Editor, Layout and Research
Beatrice W. Friel

THE POWER OF INDUSTRY

Featuring the story of Benjamin Franklin

Advisors
Paul and Millie Cheesman
Mark Ray Davis
Rodney L. Mann, Jr.
Roxanne Shallenberger
Dale T. Tingey

Publisher
Steven R. Shallenberger

Director and Correlator
Lael J. Woodbury

AN EAGLE SYSTEMS
INTERNATIONAL
PUBLICATION

ANTIOCH, CALIFORNIA

The Power of Industry
Copyright © 1981 by
Power Tales
Eagle Systems International
P.O. Box 1229
Antioch, California 94509

ISBN: 0-911712-88-7

Library of Congress Catalog No.: 81-50862

First Edition

Lithographed in USA by
COMMUNITY PRESS, INC.

A member of
The American Bookseller's Association
New York, New York

Dedicated to our young readers in the hopes that they
will be motivated to become more industrious.

BENJAMIN FRANKLIN

Benjamin Franklin was born 17 January 1706 to Josiah and Abiah Folger Franklin in a small wooden house in Boston. He was the fifteenth of seventeen children. A short time after his birth the family moved to a house where Ben's father could continue his soap and candle business on a larger scale.

At eight years of age, having already learned to read, Ben started school. But at ten he was taken out of school to help his father in his business. Ben's duties were to tend the shop, run errands, cut the wicks, and help fill the dipping and casting molds for the candles. (Cast candles were made by pouring hot tallow or wax into tin molds in which wicks had been placed. Dipped candles were made by repeatedly dipping wicks into the melted mixture.)

Ben didn't like the candle-making business and wanted to go to sea. Being afraid Ben might do this, as an older brother had already done, Ben's father took him to watch different tradesmen at work. Thus he hoped to find a trade on land that Ben would enjoy. Ben indicated later that this was a very valuable education for him.

At the age of twelve Ben went to work with his brother James in the printing business. He learned fast and became very useful. Ben also had access to a great variety of books and, as he loved to read, he would spend the greatest part of the night reading.

Ben later said that the books he had read had a great influence on his life. Among the books he felt had the greatest influence were Dr. Mather's *Essays to Do Good* and DeFoe's *Essay on Projects* (the projects were ideas for improving insurance companies, banks, asylums, roads, etc.)

Using some of his favorite books as models, Ben began writing. By the time he was sixteen, he was slipping anonymous articles under the door of his brother's print shop. Not knowing who had written them and thinking they were quite good, his brother printed them.

In 1723 Ben left his brother and went to Philadelphia, where he again worked in the printing business. Before long Ben and a friend of his opened a print shop. In 1730 Ben bought his partner's shares and became sole owner of the business, which included a newspaper.

Ben's ability to write well was a great advantage to him in the printing business and throughout his life. He not only published a popular weekly newspaper, but he also published *Poor Richard's Almanack*, which he continued to successfully publish for some twenty years.

As Ben's business grew, he purchased other printing houses. When he discovered ability and integrity among his employees, he made them partners in the businesses which he had purchased.

Ben married Deborah Read in 1730. They had two children, a son, who died as an infant, and a daughter. Ben had one other son.

Being active in civic affairs, Ben was instrumental in forming a public library, establishing an academy, and in organizing a police force, a militia, and a fire-fighting company. He worked to get streets paved and to improve street lighting. These are but a few of the many public services he rendered.

By the time Ben was forty-two, he had done well enough in the printing business to retire, which he did. He attributed his success in business to his having given superior service. Ben had always put great importance on truth, sincerity, and integrity.

Ben's retirement from business allowed him to become more actively involved in many other projects. His achievements in these other fields brought him renown as a scientist, an inventor, a patriot, a statesman, and an author.

He was active until his death, on 19 April 1790 at the age of eighty-four.

Hello there! I'm Solomon Squirrel. I must hurry to gather nuts to store for winter, but I want to stop long enough to tell you about a friend of mine. He was industrious, too. Do you know what that means?

Ants, beavers, and we squirrels are industrious. We work steadily and hard. We don't like to be idle or to waste time. We don't like to sit and watch somebody else be busy, we like to be doing things ourselves.

Well, as I was saying, this friend of mine, Benjamin Franklin, was very industrious and very hard-working. In fact, he wrote sayings like "Industry pays debts" and "God gives all things to industry."

Benjamin Franklin enjoyed being busy. He was a writer and printer, an inventor, and a fine statesman who helped our government get started. By working steadily and putting a lot of energy into his efforts, he amazed people by how much he accomplished.

Some people would look at a problem and say, "If it *could* be done, someone else would have already done it." Ben paid no attention but set to work on the problem. If he heard someone lazily say, "It needs to be done, but let someone else do it," Ben always thought *he* was that someone else.

EARLY LESSONS IN BEING INDUSTRIOUS

At the time Benjamin Franklin was born, our nation was very young. Most people had to work long hours just to eat and have a home. Not many people lived in this country, so each of them had to be more industrious. They had few luxuries and little spare time.

Ben's parents, Josiah and Abiah Franklin, lived in Boston, Massachussetts, and worked extra hard because they had so many children.

Born January 17, 1706, Ben was their fifteenth child! Later they had two more daughters.

Of course their little house was crowded, even though all the children weren't home at the same time. By the time the younger ones were born, some of the older ones had married or gone to other cities or countries to work.

Another reason they were crowded was that the big room at the front of their house was used as a soap and candle shop. That was where Ben and the other children helped their father make their living.

It was common for a family to have a shop in its home, and most children had to help with work from the time they were able. From his parents Ben probably first heard these sayings he wrote later: "Laziness travels so slowly that poverty soon overtakes him," and "At the workingman's house, hunger looks in but dares not enter."

Even as a child Ben used any free time he had to learn. He was curious about everything, and he even taught himself to read by the time he was five. He realized that the "work" of children is to learn, so they can serve others better when they are older. His parents realized Ben had special abilities, even while he was very young.

"Benjamin seems quicker than the others," his mother confided to Josiah one day. "Although he's only five, he can already read some of the Bible. We must make sure he has many chances to learn."

In those days children were not always required to go to school. They could go to work in a shop to learn a trade instead. Schools were small and bare, compared to ours. Many grades met in the same room with a single teacher. Pencils, paper, and books were expensive and scarce. Most children wrote on a slate, which was like a small blackboard. Ben had to borrow most of the books he read because only rich people had many books of their own.

Ben started attending school with his friends and studied hard. But before long Josiah said to his wife:

"I need more help from Ben. I could make more candles if he stayed with me in the shop all day."

"But he's only ten!" his mother protested. "Two years of schooling isn't enough for such a bright boy."

"I know, but his teachers say he's poor in arithmetic and only fair in writing." His father thought for a minute. "Yet, he's excellent in reading— he can learn a lot on his own."

"Maybe. He reads every book he can get his hands on—but we must also think of other ways to help him."

And they did. For years Ben had been learning all he could from traders, trappers, and sailors who came to his father's shop. As these men would talk to his dad and to each other, he'd come close and listen. The other children seemed to take little interest in the world of older people, but Ben was curious and wanted to know everything they knew!

He would even follow men from the shop and question them:

"Where have you been?"

"To London on a ship."

"What is it like to travel across the ocean? How many days did it take to go over and back? What did you see in England?"

Ben sometimes embarrassed his family by asking so many questions of strangers.

19

But his parents wanted him to learn and they thought of a plan. As talented, traveled, educated men came into their shop or visited the town, the Franklins invited them to their house for dinner. Often the family had only mush and milk at night, but when guests came, the meals were special. The parents kept the guests talking about places they'd been, things they'd seen, and books they'd read.

"Dear wife," Josiah said one evening, "a farmer came into the store today

and I invited him to dinner tomorrow night. Our boys need to learn more about the soil and how things grow."

When the farmer came, he told a story about a neighbor who talked about the crops he was going to have but was too lazy to plow. He said things like, "The sleeping fox catches no poultry," and "Plough deep, while sluggards (lazy people) sleep, and you shall have corn to sell and keep." Ben listened and remembered.

Ben worked at improving himself. He wanted to get rid of all his bad habits. One day a friend picked up a little notebook Ben carried around in his pocket. "Ben, I see here a page ruled with red ink into seven columns . . . one for each day of the week. Down the side are letters and after some of the letters are black dots. What's this all about?"

"It's very simple. I want to become a better person and I've found that just to *decide* to do right is not enough. Bad habits must be broken and replaced by good ones."

"Oh, so that's what the letters stand for!" his friend remarked.

"Exactly. Here, let me explain a few of them:

    T is for temperance (do not eat nor drink too much)

    S is for silence (speak only what may benefit others or yourself; avoid silly conversation)

    O is for order (let all your things have their place, each task its time)."

"Now I understand—R is for resolution; F is for frugality. But what's this I?"

"That stands for industry—to always be busy in doing useful things. Sometimes I find myself wasting time and doing unnecessary things."

"I see. What do the black dots mean?"

"At the end of the day I put a little black spot after each fault I have remembered."

"Do you work on all these habits at once?"

"No. I started at the top and worked a week on temperance. The second week I continued to watch myself on that but also worked on silence."

"Sounds like a pretty good system! Let me see, your list includes thirteen items. Did you master every habit in thirteen weeks?"

"No. I found I had more bad habits than I imagined. But by working at

replacing them with good habits, I *have* improved. I go through the list about four times a year."

THINK ABOUT IT

1. Ben learned some things in school, but where did he learn most of the things he knew?
2. Why should we be industrious in learning all we can when we're young?

Although Ben worked hard in his father's soap and candle shop when he was a boy, what he really wanted to do was travel and see the world. Because it was too dangerous for him to travel alone, he had to be content only to read about faraway places.

When Ben was twelve, his brother James started a print shop and hired Ben as an apprentice (that is a helper learning the trade). As Ben read the articles to be to be set in type, he thought, "I could write as well as some of these works being printed." So secretly he started writing.

When he was sixteen, his friend Tom asked him one day:

"Why don't you write something and give it to James?"

"Oh, he'd never print it if he knew I'd done it," replied Ben.

"So what could you do?" asked Tom.

Ben thought a few minutes. "Well, Tom, I could slip my piece under the print shop door at night, and I could sign it with a make-believe name."

And he did, pretending that the story was written by a widow lady, Mrs. Silence Dogood. He wrote many more articles about various problems in town—such as pigs, flies, and mud puddles in the streets. But he didn't preach in any of them. Instead, he told a clever story, as if he were on the

side of the one doing the wrong. When he explained the situation "from the backside" in an amusing way, readers saw clearly what was happening. Sometimes they got together and did something about the problem.

One day Tom asked, "Ben, how did you learn to write so well?"

"Oh, I just copy the styles of stories I've read and liked," Ben replied. Actually, the grammar and logic he had studied helped him, too.

Now you probably want to know if the real "Mrs. Silence Dogood" was discovered. Yes, he was. Ben gave it away himself, and here's how it happened.

He had Mrs. Dogood praise the cruel masters who mistreated their apprentices. As with his other stories, he had the silly lady *praise* what Ben knew was wrong, As his brother James read the story aloud, he said, "I can't print this—I'd make too many enemies among important men. Besides, I don't know whether it's true."

It was then that Ben lost his head. He said, "It is true! I know!"

"How do you know?" James questioned.

"Because I belong to a club of apprentices, and I talked with them before I wrote that story," answered Ben.

"Before what?" Oops! Ben's secret was out!

When people learned that such a young boy was writing such interesting stories, they made a great fuss over him. Even though Ben was a hard worker, James started giving him a rough time at the shop because James was jealous of the attention Ben was getting. Ben became so unhappy he

ran away to Philadelphia, then the largest city in our country. Print shops there would need helpers. He knew he was a hard worker and could get a job. Ben had a simple formula for success: *Work just a little harder than any of your competitors.*

One of his neighbors said, "That Ben Franklin is more industrious than anyone I have ever seen! I see him still at work when I go home from the club; and he's at work again before his neighbors are out of bed."

Ben worked for several printers in Philadelphia. They were happy to have someone they could trust and didn't need to push. He also traveled across the sea to London, England, and worked for printers there.

Wherever he went, whenever he had free time, he visited interesting places, questioned people about their experiences and opinions, and read. He used his spare time to learn. He wrote: "Being ignorant is not so much a shame as being unwilling to learn."

Although he hadn't been good at math in school, later he taught himself a lot about algebra and geometry, navigation, and the sciences. He wanted to be able to talk to people all over the world and to read their books, so he learned French, German, Italian, Spanish, and Latin.

You may have read some of the same books he read: *Robinson Crusoe* and *Pilgrim's Progress*. He read books written by the most well-educated men and women of his day. He knew that some people work hard not only with their hands and muscles but also with their minds.

When Ben came back from England, he bought a print shop of his own. He started his own newspaper, the Pennsylvania *Gazette*. He worked hard at informing people about what was going on in the world.

When the paper came one morning, a Mr. James Adams commented, "Ben Franklin has a clever way of bringing you over to his side of an argument."

His wife replied, "I enjoy the cartoons—I've never seen anything like them before."

Their son added, "I think it's clever how he uses maps to illustrate some of his news stories."

As time went on, Ben found he couldn't say all he wanted to say in the newspaper, so he began publishing an almanac. His almanac was a pocket-sized booklet that included many things, such as calendars and encyclopedias, holidays, tides, dates of fairs and court sessions, and forecasts of the weather.

Because books were so expensive and so many people were poor, most families had only a Bible and an almanac in their home to give them facts to help them in their work. Ben not only worked hard himself; he liked to help other people do their work in an easier and better way.

As Ben did with many of his writings, he pretended some humble person other than himself was doing the writing. Ben's little book, *Poor Richard's Almanack,* was different from other almanacs of the day. His included jokes and poems. He also included maxims—a maxim is a wise saying, often one handed down over the years. Ben gathered hundreds of them from many ages and many nations. He didn't just print them as he found them. He shortened, polished, and rearranged the words to make their meaning clear.

Some of his popular maxims include:

Work as if you were to live 100 years
Pray as if you were to die tomorrow.

The noblest [best] question in the world is,
"What good may I do in it?"

Do you love life? Then do not squander time,
for that's the stuff life is made of.

God helps them that help themselves.

About the same time Ben started his newspaper, he married Deborah Read, a lovely girl he met in Philadelphia. Later they had two boys and a girl. One of his boys died from smallpox. The other, William, grew up to become governor of New Jersey! William also learned to be industrious from his father.

THINK ABOUT IT

1. What was Ben's formula for success?
2. Why was it easy for Ben to get a job when he went to Philadelphia?
3. What do you think "God helps them that help themselves" really means?

AN INDUSTRIOUS INVENTOR AND STATESMAN

Why are people industrious? Some work hard so they can enjoy themselves by traveling, living in a fancy house, and retiring from their job early. But Benjamin Franklin worked to help *others* live better. He spent long, hard hours just solving problems that would improve life for everybody.

He didn't care about money or fame. He just enjoyed using his mind and his hands to make things better. He not only wanted to give people facts, but he wanted people to act on the facts. One time two men were talking about him:

52

"That Ben Franklin is always telling people what to do in his newspaper and his almanac," said one.

"That's true, but he wants others to find out things for themselves, not just take his word for it," replied the other.

"What makes you say that?" asked the first.

"I belong to that library he started. Each one of us members pays a little bit to buy books—then we can read them all," answered his friend.

"Say—I didn't know he was behind that! I knew he'd organized the fire department, and that he'd cleaned up the police department when he saw criminals were getting away without punishment. But I didn't know about the library."

Let's look in on a home of that day. As a little girl points to Ben Franklin's picture in the paper, she asks:

"Who's that, Mommy?"

"That's Benjamin Franklin, dear."

"Why is his picture in the paper?"

"He's being honored at a dinner tonight. Everyone in our city owes him a lot."

"Why?" asks the little girl as she curls up on her mother's lap.

"Well, before you were born, our city streets were unpaved, dirty, and dark. He thought they weren't safe, so he started a campaign to get them paved, cleaned up, and lighted."

"Is that all?"

"Isn't that enough? . . . But, no, that isn't all. If you had been born sooner, you might not have lived."

"Why not?"

"Because you needed very special care. Ben Franklin was the one who wrote, talked, and persuaded everyone to give money to build a hospital."

The little girl smiles thoughtfully, "Hmmm . . . no wonder they're giving a big dinner for him. I hope he eats a lot!"

One day as I sat on the windowsill of a schoolroom, I overheard a teacher ask the class, "What are some of the things Benjamin Franklin experimented with or invented?"

As the kids waved their hands wildly, out popped all sorts of answers:

"A stove that gives off more heat with less fuel . . ."

"Bifocal glasses—Dad wears them . . ."
"Electricity . . ."
"The lightning rod . . ."
"Ocean currents . . ."
"Daylight saving time . . ."

Later I perched on the windowsill during the history class and heard the teacher ask how Ben Franklin served his country. Again the kids knew plenty of answers:

"Sent to England to help try to avoid the Revolutionary War . . ."
"After not succeeding, returned home to help with the war . . ."
"Helped write the Declaration of Independence . . ."

"Signed it . . ."

"Went to France to ask for money and men to help fight the war . . ."

"Helped write the treaty that ended the Revolutionary War . . ."

"Helped decide what to put in the Constitution . . ."

"Kept peace in meetings when men got angry . . ."

"Signed the Constitution of the United States!"

Of course this list is just a small part of what he actually did in his busy life. This industrious man, through lifelong study and earnest, steady effort, accomplished so much it's nearly unbelievable! And he never did retire from serving in political or community affairs. He was active up until he died on April 17, 1790, at the age of eighty-four. So many people loved him that about 20,000 people attended his funeral! We owe a lot to Benjamin Franklin and his industriousness.

Well, I must get a move on. It's fun to plan ahead, to run quickly, and to be prepared. If we squirrels don't scamper around and work hard, we go hungry in the winter.

So take a tip from me—and from Benjamin Franklin—be industrious!